ABOUT THE AUTHOR

As a Soul Coaching Practitioner, business owner, and author, JK Shephard is dedicated to guiding individuals on the journey of self-discovery, empowerment, and authenticity.

A meditation specialist and passionate about self-growth and mindfulness, JK believes in the transformative power of sacred spaces — both physical and spiritual — to unlock the limitless potential within.

5 Super Powers Unleashed in Silence and Solitude: The Sacred Space Within is the culmination of their commitment, courage and vision to explore the road less traveled and to inspire others to step into their truth and live a life of power and authenticity.

Prologue

Welcome to the Journey. Within the quiet of your sacred space lies an extraordinary truth: everything you need to transform your life is already within you. Hidden beneath the noise of the world, five incredible superpowers are waiting to be unlocked—clarity, intuition, manifestation, emotional resilience, and self-mastery.

5 Superpowers Unleashed in Silence and Solitude: The Sacred Space Within is your guide to discovering the magic of stillness and the power of solitude. Through thoughtful insights, practical exercises, and timeless wisdom, this book shows you how to reconnect with your inner self and harness the transformative energy of silence.

You will learn to:

- Embrace the power of solitude to hear the whispers of your soul.
- Gain clarity on your purpose, path, and truth.
- Activate your intuition and trust its guidance.
- Manifest your desires with intention and inspired action.
- Build emotional resilience to navigate life's challenges with grace.

- Achieve self-mastery and step into your fullest potential.

This is not just a book—it is a journey into the sacred space within you. By embracing silence and solitude, you will uncover the tools to create a life of authenticity, fulfillment, and purpose.

In a world that pulls our attention outward—toward constant noise, endless responsibilities, and unrelenting distractions—the connection to our inner self often fades into the background. Yet, this connection is the key to unlocking your greatest potential, the secret to aligning with your authentic self and discovering the life you are truly meant to live.

5 Superpowers Unleashed in Silence and Solitude: The Sacred Space Within: is an invitation to pause, step back, and rediscover who you are at your core. This book serves as a guide to embarking on a transformative journey into your sacred space—a journey that leads to clarity, authenticity, and deep fulfillment.

Your sacred space is waiting. Are you ready to unlock your superpowers?

Introduction
Sacred, Space, Chronicles

Before beginning your journey, it is essential to understand the meaning and connection between three key transformative concepts explored throughout this book: **sacred**, **space**, and **chronicles.** These are not just words, but interconnected building blocks that lay the foundation for self-discovery, healing, and empowerment.

By understanding and embracing these principles, you unlock the tools to create a life of intention, growth, and profound transformation. Your journey begins with these elements as your guide, leading you toward the clarity and strength already within you.

Sacred lays the groundwork, representing the recognition of your journey as deeply meaningful and worthy of reverence. To call something sacred is to elevate its importance, to treat it with the care and intention it deserves. It is about reclaiming the divinity within yourself and honoring the unique, powerful being that you are. It is the act of creating a sanctuary—an internal space where your highest self can emerge, free from judgment, fear, or interruption.

From this hallowed, sacred place, **space** becomes the container where sacredness unfolds—a quiet environment you cultivate for peace, reflection, and transformation. More importantly, it is the mental and emotional freedom to explore, question, and evolve.

Within this sacred space, **chronicling** emerges as the act of capturing and honoring your transformation. Every experience, challenge, and triumph holds the potential for wisdom and transformation. By reflecting on these moments—through journaling and quiet introspection—you begin to craft a powerful personal narrative; weaving together the threads of your growth and authenticity, one chapter at a time.

Understanding how these elements connect allows you to approach your journey with clarity and purpose. When you embrace what is sacred, cultivate intentional space, and chronicle your growth, you establish the foundation for profound personal transformation.

This book will guide you in creating and honoring these spaces—whether through moments of solitude, meditative practices, or intentional rituals that help you connect more deeply with yourself.

The Power of Solitude and Silence

At the heart of this book lies a profound truth: within each of us is a dormant reservoir of personal power waiting to be activated. This power—your superpowers of clarity, intuition, manifestation, emotional resilience, and self-mastery—can only emerge when you commit to moments of solitude and silence.

It is in the sacred stillness of solitude that the outside world fades, and the whispers of your soul become audible. Here, you receive the clarity to see your path, the intuition to guide your steps, the vision to create your reality, and the strength to navigate life's challenges with grace.

It is in this sacred space, you step into self-mastery, bringing more light, wisdom, and love into everything you do. You become a beacon for others—a guide for those who are still lost in the noise.

This journey is not an easy one. It demands dedication, vulnerability, and a willingness to let go of distractions. It is important to keep in mind, any discomfort you may experience during your journey is temporary, but the rewards of your courage and commitment to yourself are permanent.

A Serious Question

When was the last time you were truly alone? Not just physically alone, but mentally and emotionally—completely immersed in your own thoughts, feelings, and soul?

When was the last time you turned off the noise of the world and tuned into the silence within?

For most of us, the answer is sobering. In a world filled with constant distractions—phones, jobs, relationships—it is rare to be fully present with ourselves. Yet, it is in these quiet, undisturbed moments that your dormant superpowers begin to awaken. In solitude, you reconnect with your essence, unlock your potential, and experience a profound transformation where your dreams become a reality, and your reality becomes a dream.

To embrace this sacred space is to give yourself permission to grow, evolve, and become the author of your life.

What You Will Gain From This Book?

5 Superpowers Unleashed in Silence and Solitude: The Sacred Space Within is more than a book—it is a guide, a companion, and a sacred space in itself.

Through its pages, you will:

1. Discover tools to create sacred spaces in your life, from meditative practices to reflective journaling.
2. Explore the essence of authenticity and learn how to align your life with your inner truth.
3. Learn to cultivate moments of stillness and solitude as acts of self-love.
4. Begin your own chronicles of transformation, capturing the wisdom of your journey and setting the stage for future growth.

A Commitment to Your Higher Self

By opening this book, you are making a powerful commitment—not to a fleeting resolution, but to yourself and the life you deserve. This journey is not about achieving perfection; it is about showing up, listening to your inner voice, and embracing your authentic path, one step at a time.

Your story begins here.

Chapter One
PAUSE WITH A PURPOSE
Harnessing the Power of Silence and Solitude

Silence is not an absence—it is a presence, a profound stillness that echoes with truth. Solitude is not loneliness—it is communion, a sacred meeting with the depths of your being. Together, silence and solitude hold the power to transform, to heal, and to reveal the essence of who you are.

The Seekers of Silence
Throughout history, some of the greatest spiritual authorities and visionaries have sought silence and solitude as a path to self-discovery and enlightenment. These seekers understood that in the absence of noise and distraction, the voice of the soul speaks loudest.

Jesus Christ often retreated to the wilderness, spending forty days in solitude and fasting to seek divine guidance and fortify his spiritual mission. In silence, he found clarity, purpose, and strength.

Buddha sat beneath the Bodhi tree in deep meditation, shutting out the world to focus inward. In this profound silence, he achieved enlightenment, discovering the truth of existence and the path to liberation.

Rumi, the Sufi mystic, found inspiration in silent reflection, writing, "The quieter you become, the more you are able to hear." His poetry speaks to the transformative power of tuning into the whispers of the heart.

These examples teach us that silence and solitude are not luxuries—they are necessities. They are tools for transcending the surface noise of life and connecting with the deeper truths that reside within.

> *"Your Soul Speaks a language that cannot be heard amidst the chaos of life."*

Creating Sacred Space for Your Soul
Your external environment has a profound impact on your internal state. When you intentionally create a sacred space—a quiet, undisturbed haven—you cultivate an environment where you can hear the whispers of your soul and the guidance of your higher self.

Imagine stepping into a room lit softly by candles, filled with the scent of calming incense, and free from the intrusion of the outside world. This space is not just about physical comfort; it is about energetic alignment. In such a space, the external distractions fade, and you can tune into the subtler vibrations of your inner being.

Whispers of Your Soul

Your soul speaks in a language that cannot be heard amidst the chaos of daily life. It reveals your desires, fears, and the truths you have been avoiding. In silence, these whispers become clear, guiding you toward your most authentic path.

Guidance from Your Higher Self

When you quiet the mind, you create space for your higher self to communicate. This is the part of you that is wise, infinite, and unclouded by ego. Its guidance often comes as intuition, inspiration, or a sudden knowing.

Discovering the Truth of Who You Are

Silence strips away the masks you wear for the world. Without external voices telling you who to be, you are free to ask: Who am I? What do I truly desire? What is my purpose?

In the quiet, you may uncover truths that surprise you: You may realize that some of your goals were shaped by societal expectations rather than your authentic desires. You may confront fears or limiting beliefs that have been holding you back.

You may rediscover forgotten dreams and passions that ignite your soul. This process is not always easy. Silence can bring discomfort as it forces you to face parts of yourself you have ignored. But within that discomfort lies the seed of transformation.

Silence as the Gateway to Higher Consciousness
Silence does more than help you know yourself—it connects you to higher states of consciousness. In stillness, there is no external energy to dilute your own. You become a vessel, open to receiving insight, creativity, and universal wisdom.

Pure Energy Alignment
Without the chatter of the outside world, your energy becomes aligned and coherent. This alignment allows you to tap into the collective consciousness, where answers to life's greatest questions reside.

Transcendence of Ego
Silence dissolves the ego's grip, revealing a sense of oneness with the universe. In these moments, you may feel expansive, infinite, and deeply connected to all that is.

Clarity of Thought
In silence, your thoughts slow down, making it easier to discern truth from illusion. You begin to see the motivations behind your actions and the stories you have been told about yourself and the world.

Illusions of Society
Silence exposes the constructs society places on us—the pressure to conform, the illusion of constant busyness as success, the false values that prioritize external validation over inner fulfillment. In solitude, you are free to question these constructs and redefine what matters to you.

Patterns and Conditioning

As the noise subsides, you may begin to see the patterns in your life—cycles of behavior, relationships, and thoughts that no longer serve you. With clarity comes the power to break free from these patterns and create new, empowering ones.

Embracing the Journey

The power of silence and solitude lies in their ability to ground you in the present moment while opening doors to infinite possibility. They are the gateway to authenticity, the tools for self-discovery, and the foundation of a life aligned with your higher self.

As you continue through the pages of this book, you will be guided to cultivate silence and solitude in your daily life. You will learn how to create sacred spaces, embrace stillness, and unlock the profound wisdom that already resides within you.

Your journey to unlocking your super powers begins here—in the quiet, in the stillness, and in the truth of who you are.

Chapter Two
CLARITY
Where the Chaos ends the clarity begins

Clarity is a gift born of courage. It is the light that pierces the fog, the mirror that reflects the truth, and the compass that points you toward your authentic self. But clarity does not come without effort; it is earned through the willingness to sit with discomfort, to face what you have been avoiding, and to confront the emotions that linger in the shadows of your soul.

The Discomfort of Solitude
Solitude can be unsettling. In a society that celebrates busyness and constant stimulation, being alone with your thoughts may feel alien—or even terrifying. For many, silence acts as a spotlight, illuminating emotions and fears that have long been buried under the noise of daily life.

When you first enter solitude, the discomfort can manifest in many ways:

- A racing mind that floods you with worries, regrets, or self-doubt.
- Emotional turbulence as suppressed feelings—grief, anger, or guilt—begin to surface.
- An overwhelming urge to escape, to pick up your phone, turn on the TV, or distract yourself in some way.

This resistance is natural. Your mind and ego, accustomed to constant distraction, may rebel against the stillness. But this discomfort is a sign that you are on the brink of something powerful: the clarity that comes from facing yourself.

> *"It requires courage to confront the emotions you have avoided, and honesty to acknowledge the truths you have hidden from yourself."*

Sitting with Your Thoughts

To gain clarity, you must be willing to sit with your thoughts, no matter how uncomfortable they may be. This process is not easy. It requires courage to confront the emotions you have avoided and honesty to acknowledge the truths you have hidden from yourself.

- **Acknowledging the Shadows:** In solitude, the thoughts and feelings you have buried rise to the surface. These may include unresolved grief, unacknowledged fears, or regrets you have avoided processing. While facing these emotions can be painful, it is also liberating. Only by acknowledging them can you begin to heal and move forward.
- **Observing Without Judgment:** As you sit with your thoughts, it is important to approach them with compassion rather than judgment. You are not your thoughts—they are simply reflections of past

experiences, beliefs, and conditioning. By observing them without attachment, you can begin to separate your true self from the narratives your mind has created.

- **The Power of Persistence:** The discomfort will not last forever. Like storm clouds passing across the sky, your emotions will eventually shift, leaving behind a clearer, calmer mental landscape.

The Breakthrough to Clarity

Once you move through the discomfort, something incredible begins to happen: clarity emerges. Like sediment settling at the bottom of a jar of water, your thoughts and emotions begin to organize themselves, revealing the truths hidden beneath the surface.

1. **Clarity About Your Emotions**
   By sitting with your feelings, you gain a deeper understanding of their origins and purpose. What initially feels like anger, for example, may reveal itself as unexpressed hurt. What feels like fear may point to a need for growth or change. This emotional clarity allows you to process and release what no longer serves you.
2. **Clarity About Your Patterns**
   In silence, you become aware of the habits and thought patterns that shape your life. Perhaps you notice a tendency to self-sabotage when faced with success, or a

pattern of choosing relationships that do not honor your worth. With this awareness, you can begin to break free from these cycles and create new, healthier patterns.

3. **Clarity About Your Desires**
   Without the influence of outside voices, you can finally hear your own. What do you truly want? What lights you up, excites you, or fills you with purpose? Solitude helps you separate the desires of your soul from the expectations of society, family, or peers.

4. **Clarity About Your Values**
   In the quiet, you can reconnect with your core values—the principles that define who you are and what matters most to you. This clarity empowers you to make decisions and live a life aligned with your authentic self.

The Terrifying Beauty of Truth

Clarity can be both liberating and terrifying. It often reveals truths you would rather not face: relationships that no longer serve you, habits that are holding you back, or paths that no longer align with your soul. These revelations can be painful, but they are also opportunities for growth.

As you embrace clarity, you may find yourself at a crossroads, faced with choices that require courage and change. But remember: the truth, no matter how difficult, is always a gift. It is the foundation upon which you can build a life that reflects your authentic self.

The Superpower Unleashed
When you move through the discomfort of solitude and embrace the clarity it brings, you gain a superpower: the ability to see your life, your purpose, and your path with unshakable truth. Clarity is not just a momentary insight—it is a state of being, a lens through which you can navigate the world with confidence, wisdom, and authenticity.

With clarity, you are no longer controlled by the illusions or distractions of the outside world. You see through the games society plays, the patterns that no longer serve you, and the fears that have held you back. You gain the freedom to act from a place of alignment and purpose, creating a life that resonates with your soul.

Embrace the Discomfort
Clarity does not come easily, but it is worth the effort. To gain this superpower, you must be willing to embrace the discomfort of solitude, to sit with your thoughts, and to confront the emotions you have avoided. In doing so, you will unlock a profound truth: the answers you have been seeking are already within you, waiting to be heard in the stillness. As you continue on this journey, remember that clarity is not a destination—it is a practice, a commitment to seeing yourself and your life with honesty and compassion. Each moment of solitude brings you closer to your authentic self, and with every step, you unleash more of the superpower that lies within.

When the fog of distraction and unresolved emotion lifts, your inner guidance—the quiet, knowing voice of your soul—can finally be heard. Clarity is the foundation upon which intuition is built.

Clarity sharpens your awareness, allowing you to distinguish between the chatter of fear and the whispers of truth. It clears the path for intuition to emerge as a trusted ally, guiding you with confidence and wisdom.

As you embrace the superpower of clarity, you open the door to your next transformation: the awakening of intuition, a profound connection to your higher self that leads you to make choices aligned with your deepest purpose.

The question is, are you willing to face yourself? Are you willing to confront the truth no matter how uncomfortable it may be? If so, get ready to unlock the your next super power - your *intuition*.

CHAPTER THREE
INTUITION
THE WHISPER WITHIN:
FOLLOWING THE VOICE OF YOUR SOUL

Deep within you lies another superpower, your intuition. This is your knowing voice, ever-present, ever-guiding, and always attuned to your highest good. But for many, this superpower remains dormant, drowned out by the noise of the world and the chaos of the mind. To unlock and harness this profound gift, you must first embrace solitude and silence, for it is only in stillness that intuition can truly be heard.

The Constant Whisper of Your Soul
Your intuition is always speaking to you, but it does not shout. It whispers, softly and persistently, offering insight and guidance at every turn. Unfortunately, most people cannot hear it—not because it is absent, but because they are too busy listening to everything else.

- **The Noise of the World:** The opinions of others, societal expectations, and external pressures create a cacophony that drowns out your inner voice. You may find yourself chasing goals that do not truly fulfill you or making decisions based on what others think you *should* do, rather than what feels right to you.

- **The Noise Within:** Even in moments of stillness, the fears, doubts, and judgments in your own mind can obscure your intuition. The ego, with its need for control and certainty, often overpowers the subtle, non-linear wisdom of the soul.

When you are too busy listening to these external and internal distractions, your intuition remains buried. It takes solitude and silence to clear this noise and reconnect with the truth that has always been within you.

> *"It is only when you step away from the noise of the world and create space for stillness that your intuition can come alive."*

Hearing the Voice of Intuition

When you embrace solitude, something remarkable happens: your intuition comes through loud and clear. Like tuning a radio to the right frequency, the static of the world fades, and the signal of your soul becomes unmistakable.

- **A Quiet Voice of Truth:** In solitude, your intuition may come as a soft whisper, a gut feeling, or an inexplicable sense of knowing. It does not argue or demand—it simply speaks the truth.

- **Guiding Your Steps:** This inner guidance often points you toward choices that align with your highest good, even if they defy logic or challenge your comfort zone.

- **Connecting to the Divine:** Your intuition is your direct line to the infinite wisdom of the universe. It is the voice of the Divine within you, always available to guide, support, and uplift you.

But to access this superpower, you must be willing to pause, listen, and trust.

Seeing Yourself and Others in a New Way
The superpower of intuition extends beyond decision-making—it transforms how you see yourself and the world around you. When you tap into your intuition:

- **Self-Understanding Deepens:** Your intuition reveals truths about who you are, what you need, and what brings you fulfillment. It helps you align your actions with your soul's purpose, creating a life of authenticity and meaning.

- **Empathy and Insight Expand:** Intuition allows you to understand others on a deeper level. You may sense what someone truly needs or see beyond their words to the emotions and intentions behind them. This newfound perspective fosters compassion, connection, and clarity in your relationships.

These profound shifts are only available to those who embrace solitude. In the quiet of your sacred space, you tap into the deepest, most profound aspects of your being—powers that can transform your life and the lives of those around you.

The Challenge of Trusting Intuition

Although intuition is always available to you, many people struggle to trust it. They doubt its validity, second-guess its messages, or dismiss it as irrational. This skepticism often stems from years of conditioning to rely solely on logic, reason, and external validation.

- **"That Can't Be Right":** You may find yourself questioning your intuition, especially when it challenges conventional wisdom or defies what others expect of you. This hesitation is natural, but it can prevent you from accessing the full power of this gift.

- **Learning to Trust:** Trusting your intuition requires courage. It means listening to that quiet inner voice, even when it does not make sense, even when it goes against the advice of others, and even when it pushes you into the unknown.

Unlocking the Superpower

To unlock the superpower of intuition, you must cultivate a relationship with it. This begins with creating space for solitude and silence, where your intuition can emerge without interference. From there, you can learn to recognize, trust, and act on its guidance.

1. **Practice Listening:** Set aside time each day to sit in stillness and tune into your inner voice. Notice how intuition feels—whether it comes as a physical sensation, a thought, or a sense of knowing.

2. **Take Small Steps:** Start by following your intuition in small ways—choosing a book, making a phone call, or taking a new route. As you see the positive outcomes, your trust in this inner guidance will grow.

3. **Release the Need for Logic:** Intuition often defies reason. Trust that it operates from a higher wisdom, one that sees the bigger picture and knows what is best for you in ways your mind cannot yet comprehend.

4. **Reflect and Learn:** Keep a journal of intuitive moments—times when you followed your inner voice and the results that unfolded. This practice will reinforce your confidence in this superpower.

The Gift of Intuition
Your intuition is your most profound connection to the Divine, a source of infinite wisdom that is always guiding you toward your highest good. It empowers you to make decisions aligned with your soul, navigate life with grace and confidence, and uncover truths that transcend logic and reason.

But this gift can only be accessed in solitude. It is only when you step away from the noise of the world and create space for stillness that your intuition can come alive. By embracing solitude and learning to trust this quiet voice, you unlock a superpower that has the potential to transform every aspect of your life.

In the next chapter, we will explore the superpower of *manifestation*—another extraordinary gift that flourishes in the fertile ground of silence and solitude. As intuition guides you inward, manifestation empowers you to express your authentic self outward, creating a life that reflects the truth of who you are.

Chapter Four
MANIFESTATION
The power within:
turning intentions into reality

Once you unlock clarity and intuition, something incredible begins to happen: you realize that you have the power to create your reality. This realization is both empowering and transformative. The third superpower solitude unlocks is manifestation—the ability to consciously shape your life using the creative forces of your thoughts, beliefs, and intentions.

Manifestation is not magic; it is the natural expression of your energy. Thoughts, beliefs, and intentions are not passive—they are the building blocks of your experiences. Understanding this truth allows you to step into the role of a conscious co-creator with the Divine, shaping a life aligned with your deepest desires.

Unconscious Manifestation - Life on Autopilot
For many people, manifestation happens unconsciously. Without realizing it, they create their lives based on their deepest fears, doubts, and limiting beliefs. These unconscious patterns act as invisible forces, shaping experiences in ways that feel random or uncontrollable.

- **Believing Life is Happening to You:** Most people live with the belief that life is something that happens *to* them, rather than something they are actively shaping. They see external circumstances as fixed and immutable, leaving them feeling powerless and victimized.

- **The Creative Power of Beliefs:** Every thought, every belief, and every intention you hold is like a seed planted in the fertile soil of your mind. Whether these seeds are positive or negative, they grow and manifest in your reality. For example, if you believe you are unworthy of love, you may unconsciously attract relationships that reinforce this belief.

Unconscious manifestation is like driving a car without knowing where you are going. You are always moving, but you have no control over the destination.

> *"Manifestation is not magic; it is the natural expression of your energy."*

Becoming a Conscious Creator

The superpower of manifestation is about shifting from unconscious creation to conscious co-creation. It begins with the understanding that you are not a passive participant in life —you are an active partner with the Divine, capable of bringing your desires into existence.

- **Getting Clear on Your Intentions:**
Manifestation requires clarity. You must know what you want and why you want it. Solitude provides the space to reflect on your desires, strip away external influences, and connect with your authentic dreams. In this quiet, you can set intentions that are aligned with your highest self, free from fear or doubt.

- **Aligning Your Energy with Your Desires:**
Manifestation is not simply about thinking positive thoughts—it is about aligning your entire being with what you wish to create. This means:

    - Letting go of limiting beliefs and replacing them with empowering ones.
    - Trusting that what you desire is already on its way to you.
    - Cultivating feelings of gratitude and abundance, even before your desires have manifested.

- **Listening to Your Intuition:**
Your intuition serves as a guide in the manifestation process. It provides the insights and nudges you to take inspired action. Solitude is essential because it allows you to tune into this inner guidance without the interference of outside voices.

- **Taking Inspired Action:**
Manifestation is not a passive process. While your thoughts and beliefs set the foundation, it is your actions that bring

your desires into reality. Inspired action is different from busywork—it flows naturally, feels aligned, and is guided by intuition.

What Are You Manifesting Right Now?
Whether you realize it or not, you are always manifesting. Every thought, every belief, every intention you hold is shaping your reality in this very moment. The question is not *if* you are manifesting—it is *how*.

Manifesting from a Place of Power
When you manifest consciously, you align your energy with your desires, trust your intuition, and take inspired action. You become a deliberate creator, shaping a life that reflects your dreams and values.

Manifesting from a Place of Fear
When you manifest unconsciously, your life is shaped by limiting beliefs, self-doubt, and fear. This often leads to experiences that reinforce feelings of lack, struggle, or dissatisfaction.

Take a moment to reflect: What are you manifesting right now? Are your thoughts, beliefs, and actions aligned with the life you want to create or are they rooted in fear and doubt? The truth is, you have the power to shift at any moment.

The Role of Solitude in Manifestation

Solitude is the fertile ground where manifestation begins. Without the space to reflect and recalibrate, it is nearly impossible to manifest consciously. Solitude offers you the opportunity to:

- **Get Clear on What You Want:** Away from the distractions of the world, you can focus on your true desires without external influence.

- **Align Your Energy:** In the quiet, you can release resistance, let go of negative beliefs, and cultivate a mindset of abundance and gratitude.

- **Hear Your Intuition:** With no competing voices, your intuition becomes a trusted guide, helping you navigate the manifestation process with ease.

- **Take Aligned Action:** Solitude gives you the clarity and confidence to take inspired steps toward your goals, free from doubt or hesitation.

The Truth of Manifestation
Manifestation is not about hoping for the best or simply thinking positive thoughts. It is about stepping into your power as a co-creator with the Divine. It is about consciously choosing your thoughts, beliefs, and actions to align with the life you want to create.

This superpower is available to everyone, but it requires awareness, discipline, and trust. As you cultivate clarity and intuition through solitude, you unlock the ability to manifest with intention and purpose. You begin to see that life is not something that happens to you—it is something you create.

Manifestation Leads to Emotional Resilience

Manifestation teaches you to trust the process, to release attachment to outcomes, and to remain steadfast in the face of challenges. It builds your ability to navigate life's ups and downs with grace and confidence. As you master the art of manifestation, you will notice another superpower awakening within you: *emotional resilience*.

In the next chapter, we will explore this fourth superpower and how it empowers you to live with strength, courage, and unwavering faith in yourself and your connection to the universe.

Chapter Five
EMOTIONAL RESILIENCE
FACING YOUR FEELINGS. FINDING YOUR POWER.

As you master the art of manifestation, you unlock the next profound superpower: emotional resilience. While it may not sound as glamorous as intuition or manifestation, emotional resilience is arguably one of the most transformative and empowering abilities you can cultivate. It is the anchor that keeps you steady in the storms of life, the quiet strength that allows you to navigate challenges with grace, and the inner calm that helps you face even the most difficult emotions head-on.

Confronting Emotions in Solitude
Solitude is the crucible where emotional resilience is forged. In the stillness, there is nowhere to run, nowhere to hide from your feelings. Without distractions or external noise, you are forced to sit with your emotions, to feel them fully and deeply. This can be one of the most challenging aspects of solitude—but it is also one of the most transformative.

- **No Escape from Feelings:** Unlike in the busy rush of daily life, solitude does not offer an easy escape. You cannot numb your emotions with social media, work, relationships, or substances. You are left with only yourself and the raw truth of what you feel.

- **The Power of Sitting With Discomfort:** Facing your emotions head-on can be uncomfortable, even painful. But it is precisely in this discomfort that resilience is born. When you sit with your sadness, fear, or pain without running away, you build the strength to endure and process those emotions.

Most people avoid this process, choosing instead to suppress or distract themselves from their emotions. But true growth and resilience come only when you are willing to face what you feel, to allow your emotions to exist without resistance.

> *"Emotional resilience is not about never feeling pain—it is about being unafraid to feel."*

The Courage to Feel

To unlock emotional resilience, you must be willing to feel your emotions fully. This is not about wallowing in negativity or getting stuck in pain—it is about allowing yourself to experience your emotions without judgment or fear.

- **Emotions Are Energy:** At their core, emotions are simply energy in motion. They are not permanent or fixed; they are waves of energy moving through your body. When you allow yourself to feel them without resistance, they lose their power over you and eventually pass through you.

- **The Trap of Suppression:** Suppressing emotions does not make them go away. It only pushes them deeper into your subconscious, where they can manifest as stress, anxiety, disease, and even a pain-body. Facing your emotions, on the other hand, allows you to release them and free yourself from their grip.

- **The Freedom of Acceptance:** Emotional resilience is not about never feeling pain—it is about being unafraid to feel. When you accept your emotions as a natural part of the human experience, they lose their power to control or overwhelm you.

Are You Willing to Face Your Emotions?

Unlocking emotional resilience requires courage. You must be willing to sit with the discomfort, to feel the fear, the sadness, the loss, or the anger without running away. Ask yourself:

- Am I willing to sit with my pain and let it move through me?
- Can I accept my emotions without judgment or resistance?
- Am I ready to let go of the distractions and face what I feel?

This is not an easy path, but it is a necessary one. By confronting your emotions, you reclaim your power. You begin to see that your emotions are not your enemy—they are simply messengers, pointing you toward healing, growth, and self-understanding.

The Transformation of Emotional Resilience

When you embrace your emotions, you unlock a profound transformation. Emotional resilience is not about eliminating negative emotions—it is about learning to move through them with strength and grace. This superpower brings many gifts:

1. **Strength in Adversity:** You gain the ability to remain grounded and centered, even in the face of life's challenges. You are no longer shaken by every wave of emotion or external circumstance.

2. **Emotional Freedom:** By facing your emotions, you free yourself from their hold. You are no longer ruled by fear, sadness, or anger. Instead, you move through these emotions with confidence and ease.

3. **Deeper Self-Understanding:** Emotional resilience allows you to understand your feelings and the patterns behind them. This self-awareness fosters greater compassion for yourself and others.

Solitude as the Gateway to Emotional Resilience

Without solitude, emotional resilience is nearly impossible to cultivate. The distractions of the outside world make it all too easy to avoid your feelings. Solitude, however, provides the space and stillness necessary to confront and process your emotions.

- **The Gift of Stillness:** In solitude, you can sit with your emotions without interference. You have the time and space to explore what you feel, why you feel it, and what your emotions are trying to teach you.

- **The Power of Presence:** Solitude helps you cultivate presence, the ability to stay in the moment and fully experience what is happening within you. This presence is essential for emotional resilience, as it allows you to move through emotions without being overwhelmed.

From Resilience to Mastery

As you master emotional resilience, you unlock the ability to live with greater peace, strength, and authenticity. This superpower transforms not only how you navigate your own emotions but also how you relate to others and the world around you.

And as you continue this journey, you will discover that emotional resilience is the bridge to the ultimate superpower: *self-mastery.* In the next chapter, we will explore how the power of solitude enables you to step into full alignment with your highest self, achieving the kind of inner mastery that transforms every aspect of your life.

Emotional resilience is not just a skill—it is a way of being, a quiet strength that empowers you to face anything life brings your way. By embracing your emotions and allowing them to move through you, you become unshakable, unstoppable, and undeniably free.

Chapter Six
SELF MASTERY
Master yourself, master your life

Self-mastery is the ultimate superpower, the pinnacle of personal growth, and the culmination of the journey into solitude. It is the ability to rise above the lower aspects of yourself—the fear, the doubt, the ego—and align with your highest self. Self-mastery allows you to take control of your thoughts, your emotions, your actions, and ultimately, your destiny. It is not just about living; it is about living with intention, purpose, and power.

What is Self-Mastery?
At its core, self-mastery is the ability to govern your inner world. It means no longer being a prisoner to reactive emotions, racing thoughts, or external circumstances. It is stepping into the role of creator and taking full responsibility for your life.

- **Mastering Your Mind:** Recognizing that you are not your thoughts. You are the observer of your thoughts, the conscious presence that chooses which thoughts to entertain and which to release.

- **Mastering Your Emotions:** Understanding that emotions are not meant to control you—they are meant to be felt, understood, and released. Emotional mastery allows you to respond to life with wisdom rather than react impulsively.

- **Mastering Your Actions:** Aligning your behavior with your values and intentions, even when it is difficult. Self-mastery empowers you to act from a place of authenticity and integrity, regardless of external pressures.

Self-mastery is not about perfection. It does not mean you will never feel fear or doubt, or that you will never make a mistake. It means recognizing when these arise and consciously choosing to align with your higher self rather than being ruled by them.

> *"I am no longer a prisoner to reactive emotions, racing thoughts, or external circumstances."*

Why Solitude is Essential for Self-Mastery
Self-mastery cannot be achieved in the chaos of daily life. It requires the stillness, space, and introspection that only solitude can provide.

- **Observing Yourself:** In solitude, you have the opportunity to become a witness to your own mind. You can observe your thoughts, patterns, and behaviors without judgment, gaining valuable insights into who you are and who you want to become.

- **Reflecting on Your Choices:** Solitude gives you the space to reflect on your actions and decisions, to ask yourself whether they align with your values and your higher self.

- **Making Conscious Choices:** Without the distractions of the outside world, you can make intentional decisions about how you want to show up in life, rather than reacting to circumstances out of habit or fear.

Solitude is the sacred ground where self-mastery takes root. It is the space where you shed the layers of conditioning and reconnect with the truth of who you are.

The Process of Transformation

Self-mastery is not achieved overnight. It is a lifelong journey, requiring discipline, commitment, and a willingness to face yourself. The process can be uncomfortable, but it is in this discomfort that transformation occurs.

- **Facing the Mind:** Your mind may race with fears, doubts, or endless distractions. Rather than running from these thoughts, self-mastery requires you to stay with them, to breathe through the discomfort, and to gently guide your mind back to stillness.

- **Embracing Your Emotions:** Emotions will bubble up—pain, fear, sadness, anger. Instead of suppressing or avoiding them, you must allow yourself to feel them fully. This is not a sign of weakness; it is a step toward strength and freedom.

- **Resisting the Urge to Distract:** When challenges arise, the temptation to escape into distractions—social media, work, relationships, activities, substances—can be strong. But self-mastery demands presence. It requires you to sit with whatever arises, to breathe, and to allow yourself to simply be.

Each moment you choose to stay present with yourself, you grow stronger. Each time you align with your higher self, you move closer to mastery.

The Gifts of Self-Mastery

As you spend more time in solitude and commit to the journey of self-mastery, you will begin to notice extraordinary changes in your life.

1. **Connection to Self:** You will feel more deeply connected to yourself—your intuition, your purpose, your truth. This connection will become your guiding light, helping you navigate life with clarity and confidence.

2. **Alignment with Your Highest Self:** You will begin to rise above fear, doubt, and ego, choosing instead to align with your higher self. This alignment will bring a sense of peace and fulfillment that cannot be shaken by external circumstances.

3. **Manifestation with Ease:** With clarity and intuition as your foundation, manifestation becomes effortless. You

will align your energy with your desires and watch as the universe responds in kind.

4. **Emotional Resilience:** You will develop the strength to face any emotion, any challenge, with grace and composure. You will no longer fear your emotions—they will become tools for growth and transformation.

5. **True Power:** Most importantly, you will step into a place of true power. Self-mastery allows you to live intentionally, to create your life rather than react to it, and to move through the world with confidence, authenticity, and purpose.

The Ultimate Superpower

Self-mastery is not just about controlling your mind, emotions, or actions—it is about mastering your energy and aligning with your higher self. It is about becoming the creator of your reality, living in harmony with the Divine, and stepping into the fullness of who you are meant to be.

This superpower is not accessible to everyone. It requires discipline, courage, and a willingness to face yourself. But for those who commit to the journey, the rewards are infinite.

Living from a Place of Power

As you continue on the path of self-mastery, you will begin to notice a profound shift in your life. You will no longer feel controlled by your thoughts, emotions, or circumstances. Instead, you will feel empowered, grounded, and aligned.

- You will trust your intuition more deeply, following its guidance even when it defies logic.
- You will manifest your desires with clarity and ease, creating a life that reflects your highest purpose.
- You will face life's challenges with resilience and strength, knowing that you have the power to overcome anything.
- You will live from a place of authenticity, truth, and inner peace.

This is the gift of self-mastery: the freedom to live as the highest version of yourself, fully aligned with your purpose, your truth, and the Divine.

The Journey Ahead

The journey of self-mastery is a lifelong commitment, one that deepens with every moment of solitude and self-reflection. It is not about perfection; it is about presence. It is about choosing, moment by moment, to align with your higher self, to live with intention, and to create a life of meaning and purpose.

As you continue on this path, remember that every step you take is a step closer to your true self. Embrace the process, trust the journey, and know that the ultimate superpower of self-mastery is already within you, waiting to be unlocked.

You have all the tools you need. Now is the time to rise into your power and become the master of your mind, your emotions, your actions, and your destiny.

Chapter Seven
THE SACRED SPACE WITHIN
Choosing solitude, finding freedom

Solitude is not isolation. It is not about cutting yourself off from the world or retreating into loneliness. In fact, solitude is the opposite: it is about deep connection—to yourself, to others, and to the universe.

When you embrace solitude, you step into the sacred space where your true self resides. You unlock the superpowers that have always been within you and begin to show up in the world as a brighter, wiser, and more loving version of yourself.

This is the paradox of solitude: the more you go inward, the more you expand outward. The more deeply you connect with yourself, the more deeply you can connect with others. Solitude does not separate you from the world; it transforms the way you engage with it.

Becoming a Beacon of Light
When you align with your true self and unlock your superpowers—clarity, intuition, manifestation, emotional resilience, and self-mastery—you begin to radiate an energy that others can feel. You show up in the world differently:

- **With Greater Presence:** You are fully grounded in the moment, no longer distracted by the noise of your mind or the world. This presence brings peace and calm to those around you.

- **With Greater Compassion:** Understanding your own journey helps you empathize with others who are still struggling to find their way. You become a source of comfort, inspiration, and guidance.

- **With Greater Love:** The love you cultivate for yourself in solitude naturally spills over into your relationships, your work, and everything you do.

You become a beacon—a light for those who are lost in the noise, a guide for those searching for meaning, and a reminder of what is possible when you embrace the path of solitude and self-discovery.

> *"Solitude is not about isolation. It is about a deep connection with yourself, with others around you, and the universe."*

The Superpowers Within You

The truth is, you have always had these superpowers. They have been within you all along, waiting to be awakened. Clarity, intuition, manifestation, emotional resilience, and self-mastery are not gifts given to a select few—they are the natural abilities of every human being. But to access them, you must create the space to connect with yourself. You must step into solitude to hear the whispers of your soul, to feel the truth of your emotions, and to remember who you truly are. Solitude is not a luxury—it is a necessity for unlocking the incredible potential that lies within you.

The Courage to Walk the Path

The path of solitude is not an easy one. It requires courage to face yourself, commitment to stay the course, and a willingness to step into the unknown. There will be moments of discomfort, moments when you want to turn back, moments when the noise of the world feels easier than the stillness within.

But it is also the most rewarding path you can walk. It is the path that leads to:

- **True Power:** The ability to master your thoughts, emotions, and actions, and to create a life aligned with your highest self.

- **True Freedom:** Freedom from the expectations of others, the illusions of society, and the limitations of fear and doubt.

- **True Fulfillment:** The deep satisfaction that comes from living authentically, guided by your intuition and aligned with your purpose.

The rewards of this journey far outweigh its challenges. Every step you take brings you closer to the truth of who you are and the life you are meant to live.

The Choice is Yours

Now, the choice is yours. Will you continue to distract yourself with the noise of the world, or will you step into the stillness and unlock the superpowers that are waiting for you?

- Will you choose to create a sacred space for yourself, to pause, and to listen?
- Will you choose to face your emotions, your fears, and your doubts with courage and compassion?
- Will you choose to walk the path of solitude, even when it feels uncomfortable, knowing that it leads to your greatest potential?

The path is open. The pause is powerful. All you have to do is embrace it.

Everything You Have Been Searching For

Remember, everything you have been searching for has been within you all along. The clarity, the wisdom, the strength, the love—it is already there, waiting for you to notice it. Solitude is the key that unlocks the door.

- In the stillness, you will find your truth.
- In the quiet, you will hear the voice of your soul.

- In the sacred space of solitude, you will remember who you truly are.

The path to your highest self is not somewhere out there. It begins within you, in the moments of silence, in the courage to pause, and in the willingness to embrace solitude.

Are You Ready?
The choice is yours. Are you ready to walk the path? Are you ready to embrace solitude, to face yourself, and to unlock the superpowers that have been waiting for you?

If you are, then step into the stillness. Embrace the pause. Trust the process. And remember:

You are the light. You are the creator. You are the master of your destiny.

The journey begins now.

Chapter Eight
THE CHRONICLES
Capturing growth. Unlocking wisdom

As you come to the end of this book, you have taken an incredible step toward unlocking the superpowers that lie within you. You have explored the transformative power of silence and solitude, uncovering tools for clarity, intuition, manifestation, emotional resilience, and self-mastery.

This is no small feat—it is a courageous journey that will continue to unfold as you embrace these practices in your daily life. But transformation does not happen in isolation. One of the most powerful ways to deepen your journey is through journaling, a practice that allows you to capture your thoughts, process your emotions, and reflect on your growth.

Journaling creates a bridge between your inner world and the physical one, helping you bring clarity to your insights and intentionality to your actions.

To support you in this ongoing journey, I have created a series of Journals: **Sacred Space Chronicles**, designed to supplement your moments of silence with personal growth and reflection.

Each journal is tailored to guide you through specific areas of self-discovery and transformation, making them the perfect companions to your sacred space practice.

- **A Positive Mind-Set Journal:** Transform your mind, transform your life. Reframe challenges, cultivate optimism, and shift your perspective to see the possibilities in every situation.
- **Calming Your Mind Journal**: Master your mind, master yourself. Cultivate mindfulness and patience to navigate life with greater ease, presence and peace.
- **Discover Yourself Journal:** Embrace the wisdom within. Dive deep into who you are, uncovering your authentic self and aligning with your purpose.
- **Gratitude and Appreciation Journal**: Unlock abundance. Focus on the blessings in your life and cultivate a mindset of abundance and joy.
- **Healing and Self-Compassion Journal:** Transform pain into purpose and passion. Embrace self-kindness, release emotional wounds, and nurture a stronger, more resilient you
- **Inner-Child Healing Journal:** Heal the child, empower the adult. Nurture your inner-chile to rediscover joy, resilience, and authenticity.
- **Let That Sh*t Go Journal**: Forgive, release, reflect, and reclaim your peace.

- **Self-Love Journal**: Embrace yourself, empower the world. Build a stronger relationship with yourself and others, embracing self-compassion and acceptance.
- **Self-Reflection Journal**: Know yourself, grow yourself. Deepen your connection with yourself through thoughtful reflection and meaningful insights.

Access Your Free Guidebook

To help you get started, I have created a free resource: ***The Sacred Space Chronicles Guidebook: A Journey to Authenticity.*** This guidebook explains the power of journaling and how it can be used as a tool for personal growth, clarity, and transformation.

Take the Next Step

Your journey does not end here—it is only beginning. The superpowers you have unlocked in silence and solitude are just the start. By chronicling your practice, you can amplify your growth, maintain your connection to your higher self, and continue creating a life of purpose and fulfillment.

Visit ***https://sacredspace-vision.b12sites.com*** to explore the **Sacred Space Journals** and claim your free guidebook today.

Your next chapter awaits.

Made in United States
Orlando, FL
20 January 2025

57507440R00039